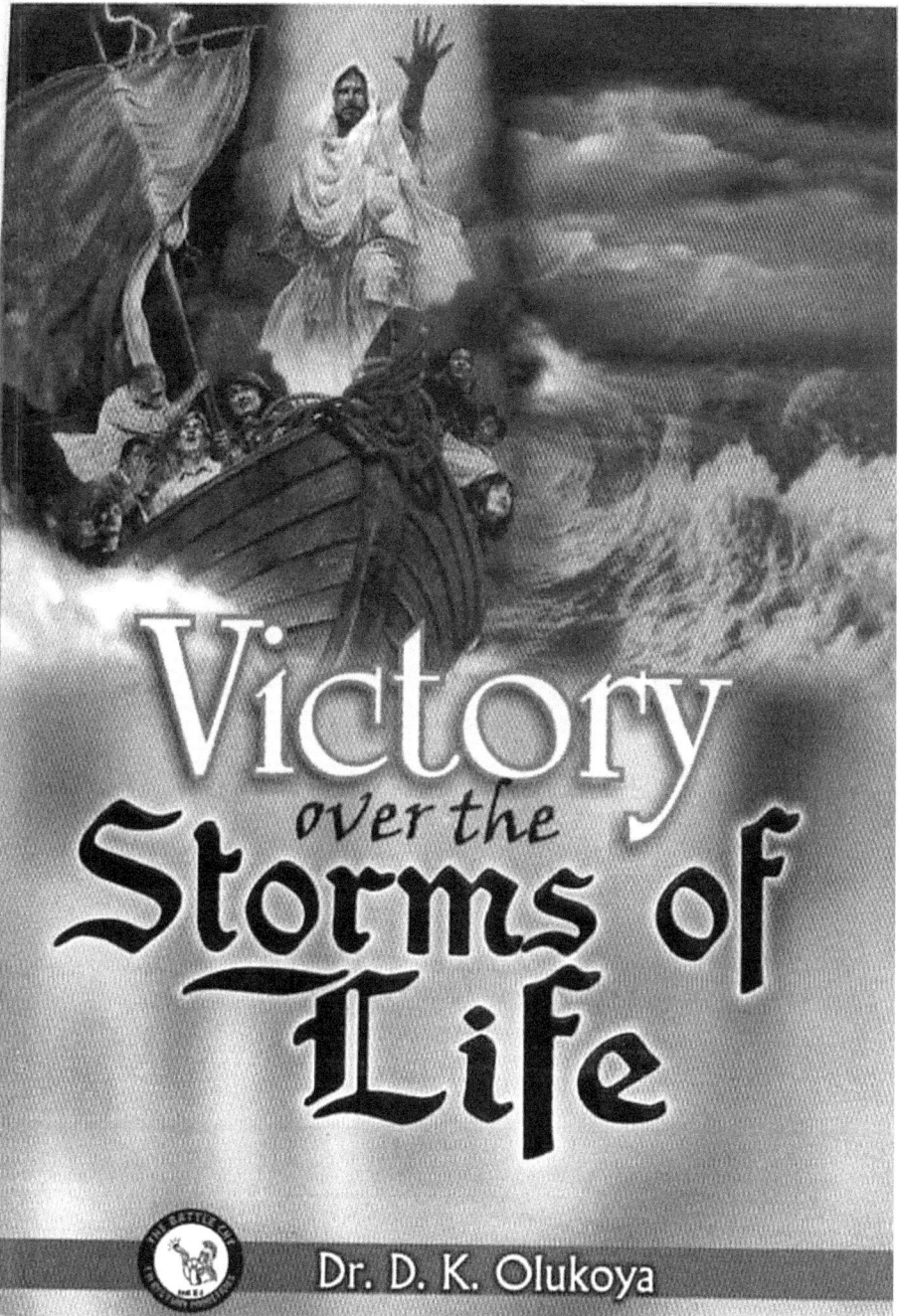

Victory
over the
Storms of
Life

Dr. D. K. Olukoya

Victory
OVER THE
STORMS
OF LIFE

DR. D. K. OLUKOYA

VICTORY OVER THE STORMS OF LIFE
© 2012 DR. D. K. OLUKOYA
ISBN: 978-978-920-039-9
Published - September 2012 AD

Published by:
The Battle Cry Christian Ministries

322, Herbert Macaulay Street, Sabo, Yaba
P.O. Box 12272, Ikeja, Lagos
www.battlecrystore.com,
email: info@battlecrystore.com ,
        customercare@battlecrystore.com,
        sales@battlecrystore.com,
Phone: 0803-304-4239, 01-8044415

I Salute my wonderful wife, Pastor Shade, for her invaluable support in the ministry.
I appreciate her unquantifiable support in the book ministry as the cover designer, art editor and art adviser.

All the scriptures are from the King James Version.

Contents

CHAPTER	PAGE
1. VICTORY OVER THE STORMS OF LIFE	4
2. YOUR STORMS AND YOUR BATTLES	17
3. CLASSIFICATION OF STORMS	24
4. PROVOKING YOUR RAINFALL	33

CHAPTER One

Victory Over the STORMS OF LIFE

A storm is a strong, destructive wind. The Bible uses the word to describe the problems of life. A storm is also defined as a very bad weather, with strong winds, rain and thunder. It refers to the distresses, troubles, calamities, frustrations and turbulences of life.

The world is hit by different storms everyday. There are storms of sicknesses and incurable diseases. There are storms of poverty, war, battles, conflicts, destructions, disasters and losses. Confusion can blow strongly like a storm. Opposition can be a storm. Persecutions and financial crises are also common storms of life. Looking at all these, you see that the world is full of storms. Unbelievers have their kinds of storms and the children of God are not free from the storms of life either. But God delivers His own from every storm of life.

> *Many are the afflictions of the righteous: but the LORD delivereth him out of them all. He keepeth all his bones: not one of them is broken.* **Ps 34: 19-20.**

AFFLICTIONS OF THE RIGHTEOUS

Another Bible word for storm is affliction. The verses above introduce us to all the afflictions of the righteous, not just one or two. There was no righteous man in the Bible days who did not experience one form of affliction or another. It is not a strange thing to be going through troubles as a child of God. The word of God says the afflictions of the righteous are many.

Many Christians don't understand the mind and providence of God. They think it is strange to suffer afflictions in the world. But it is not strange. Those who were righteous before you had their own storms.

The storms of life do not come because of sin or unrighteousness. If you don't prepare your heart against the days of storms, you may lose your balance when they come upon you. Christians often talk about troubles breaking loose on them unawares. Such confession only shows that many of us are not prepared for storms or expect they could blow upon us.

My brethren, count it all joy when ye fall into divers temptations; James 1:2.

YOUR ATTITUDE

The Christian's attitude to the storms of life should be different from the attitude of those who don't know God. There is a way God wants you to react and respond to the storms of life. Many times, our storms are not as bad as the way we face them or the attitude we exhibit towards them. Because of storms, you find people losing their commitment to the Lord. Because of storms, you find Christians losing their virtues. Because of storms, you find believers seeking alternative solutions from wrong persons and places. God never allows us to go through any storm that would ruin us. If we realise He is there to weather our storms, we will be calm in our dependence on Him when the storms blow.

Immediately the Bible talks about the many afflictions of the righteous, it brings God's deliverance near as much as possible. In the same verse where it talks about the many afflictions of the righteous, the Bible also reveals that the God of the righteous would deliver His own. There is a righteous God in heaven who delivers the righteous in the world. The righteousness of God does not permit Him to overlook or abandon the righteous in their storms. If you sink in the storms of life, it is because you fail to realise how close God is to you.

DELIVERANCE IS SURE!

The last part of verse 19 of the references above is very interesting. It is a tonic to our blood and a marrow to our bones. As the afflictions of the righteous are many, so are the deliverances of God. As storms blow upon the righteous from different directions, so God has different methods of delivering His people. He does not deliver us from just some storms and afflictions but delivers us from all of them. Verse 20 of the passage concludes by saying that when He delivers us, we are preserved.

God delivers from afflictions and keeps His own. Only God can deliver you from all your afflictions and preserve you without hurt. That is what the Bible means when it says God keeps our bones.

He keepeth all his bones: not one of them is broken. **Psalm 34:20.**

GOD IS NEAR

Settle it in your mind that you will experience afflictions in this world. Know it in your heart that this is a world of troubles. But above these, be very sure in your heart that in all your afflictions, God is near to deliver you. Don't be narrow-minded to think that your storms are so peculiar that even God cannot help. If help fails to come from God, where will you get it? God delivers from all afflictions.

They mount up to the heaven, they go down again to the depths: their soul is melted because of trouble. They reel to and fro, and stagger like a drunken man, and are at their wits' end. Then they cry unto the LORD in their trouble, and he bringeth them out of their distresses. He maketh the storm a calm, so that the waves thereof are still. Then are they glad because they be quiet; so he bringeth them unto their desired haven. Oh that men would praise the LORD for his goodness, and for his wonderful works to the children of men! Ps 107:26-31.

The children of Israel had storms. They went through overwhelming troubles. They suffered fierce afflictions. The psalmist looked back to the pilgrimage of the older generations of Israel and saw God's deliverances and providence spread out in all their experiences. If you look at your own life very well, you will see the invisible hands of God, always working out your salvation from destructions, your deliverances from afflictions and your safety in times of storms. Just look but make sure you look at your life very well. God has never been far away from His own people.

THE HURRICANE

If the psalmist did not refer to the children of Israel in the Scripture above, we are likely to think about what happened to unbelievers. Troubles beat high against them. He said it was like watching a large assembly of people, taken up by a strong wind of troubles. The children of Israel found themselves in storms that took them from their level of control and human experiences. As eagles mount up with wings in adverse winds, so troubles blew them high above the earth.

What the psalmist is describing here is very serious. You must have seen papers and other light materials blown by strong winds, especially when it is about to rain. You look through your window and find the sky filled with flying objects taken up in the storm. Up there, they have no specific direction. While they are being whirled in the sky, they cannot determine where they would land. Hence, you find an object taken up in the wind from one part of town to another. In some cases, some articles are blown away, completely out of sight. The storms take them from one town, city, or state to another.

A TRAUMATIC EXPERIENCE

As you imagine this in your heart, compare the children of Israel to these articles in the winds. The psalmist said that was what their storms did to them. They were taken up, drifted and wouldn't know where they would land. It was a state of confusion. It was an experience that defied human wisdom. It was an experience where collective efforts could not deliver them. They had storms which melted their souls.

True to what the psalmist said, as earlier seen in chapter 34, God delivered them from their afflictions. Their storm made them look like drunkards as they lost control. Have you seen a drunkard staggering to find his way? This should make you know that troubles can be so strong as to make a man of strength stagger as though he knew not what to do. The children of Israel moved to and fro because they had no direction in their afflictions. They ran forward and backwards. They were desperate to get a solution.

These are some of the things believers experience in the time of storms. That you lost control of your situation when the storm blew does not mean you are not a believer. The children of Israel were still God's covenant people, but they lost control in their storm. You could lose direction in your storm. One of the experiences of sailors in those days was loss of direction when storms raged. That you lost proper direction in your storm does not reduce you as a believer. Your experiences are only evidence that you had storms.

THE EVERLASTING POWER

For us to know that the deliverance of God is near His own, the psalmist said that the children of Israel cried out to God and their situation changed. God brought them out of their distresses, calmed their storms and made the waves of their troubles to become still. When all of man's wisdom fails to calm a storm, there is wisdom with God to do the impossible. When all strength wane in troubles, there is everlasting power with God to save and to deliver. Hence, there is the need to trust Him as

His word says:

> *When thou passest through the waters, I will be with thee; and through the rivers, they shall not overflow thee: when thou walkest through the fire, thou shalt not be burned; neither shall the flame kindle upon thee.*
> Isa 43:2.

Facing the troubles of life is like passing through the waters. These troubles can be so strong as to make them look as if we were passing through a river. Passing through the affliction of life is like passing through a fire that burns. In them all, God delivers the righteous so that they go through them unhurt.

> *And the same day, when the even was come, he saith unto them, Let us pass over unto the other side. And when they had sent away the multitude, they took him even as he was in the ship. And there were also with him other little ships. And there arose a great storm of*

> *wind, and the waves beat into the ship, so that it was now full. And he was in the hinder part of the ship, asleep on a pillow: and they awake him, and say unto him, Master, carest thou not that we perish? And he arose, and rebuked the wind, and said unto the sea, Peace, be still. And the wind ceased, and there was a great calm.* **Mark 4:35-39.**

THE DIVINE STRATEGY

Jesus faced storms with His disciples. He gave an instruction that they should cross over to the other side of the river. Having said so, He fell asleep on a pillow and the storms began to rage. Let me tell you something: God has a way of deceiving the enemies to waste their powers against His children. Jesus was asleep when the waters began to rage. Have you ever thought about why the storm did not rage while He was awake?

There are times God creates room for the enemies to rage. He makes it look as if He was far or was not seeing you. There is no vacuum in creation because God filled all of it. Even when it does not look like He is there, He is, and would always be there.

Though Jesus was asleep, the fact remains that He was there! The power of God is right with you to deliver. That is why the psalmist said; "Let God arise." God could sit down quietly and be still. That is why the psalmist said, "Stir thyself out of thy holy temple." Even when it looks as if God was far away during your storms, He is not. He is there at all times.

Prayer Points

1. Every power prolonging affliction in my life, I bury you today in Jesus name.

2. Every problem expander, I kill you power today in Jesus Name.

   I Shall go from glory to glory, and strength to strength in Jesus Name

. The enemy will not measure my length on the ground in name of Jesus.

'. Holy Ghost, arise and deliver me from every evil cage in the name of Jesus.

ɔ. I decree an end to every witchcraft affliction in Jesus name.

7. I must experience total deliverance by the power in the blood of Jesus.

8. Every lion of death, crouching to attack me die in Jesus name.

9. Thou power of backwardness, lose your power, in Jesus name.

10. By the thunder of your power, O Lord kill the power behind my problem in Jesus name.

11. Let the finger of God arise and disgrace every powe working against my peace in the name of Jesus.

12. Let your angel arise, O Lord and cut-off every umbilical cord of sorrow, in the name of Jesus.

13. I dismantle every chain-problem in the name of Jesus name.

14. Every power magnetizing any problem to me loose your hold, in the name of Jesus name.

15. I must arise and shine in the name of Jesus name.

CHAPTER Two

Your Storms and your BATTLES

The totality of your battles in life is made up of storms that occur at various points in your experience. In this chapter, we shall examine how storms affect our battles in life. Take note of these seven vital points:

FACTS ABOUT STORMS

1. Storms are situations resulting in stress in our lives.

2. Storms are crises of life.

3. They represent what the Bible calls "the time of Jacob's troubles."

4. They represent what Jesus described as "the hour of darkness."

5. They are when things go wrong dramatically.

6. They are like journeys through the valley of the shadow of death.

7. They are in place when the seven "Ds" of life have taken over. What are these "Ds?"
   (a) Doubt,
   (b) Distress,
   (c) Disappointment,
   (d) Depression,
   (e) Discouragement,
   (f) Disillusionment and
   (g) Defeat.

Life is like a machine in constant motion. It either grinds or polishes, depending on your attitude to it. The sun that melts the candle is the same sun that hardens the clay. The real man or woman is the one who is steadfast in the face of trouble. The harder your conflict as a child of God, the more glorious your victory.

NO BATTLE, NO PROGRESS

There can never be progress without a battle. Nothing has ever moved ahead normally without a battle or without a conflict. Difficulties are the forerunners of greatness. Passing through hard times will give you spiritual muscles you will need later in life. A smooth sea does not produce a skilled sailor. A good pilot is known for his worth during storms. Life always goes forward, only human beings go backward.

Move forward in your storms! Moses and the children of Israel were caught between mountains and were trapped between the Red Sea and the Egyptians. Moses cried out to God and the Lord told him to move forward. Storms cannot stop you except you allow them. Afflictions cannot turn you away from God except you give up.

> And Moses cried unto the LORD, saying, What shall I do unto this people? they be almost ready to stone me. Ex 17:4.

Many opportunities come in different ways but they disguise as impossible situations. Those who know their God will move forward, not minding the situations of life. Life itself is a mystery we cannot fully comprehend here on earth. There are powers that govern the universe. If you fail to understand these mysteries, you will fail to grasp the truth about the ordinances that make the heavens and the earth. Failure to understand these is ultimate failure in life.

DIFFERENT STROKES

Whatever experience you are passing through now, somebody somewhere has passed through it before without dying. Therefore, no problem can kill you. Take this prayer point now:

"No problem shall kill me, in the name of Jesus."

The battles validate the fact that, "One man's meat is another man's poison." Your most important desire may be very harmful to the desire of another person.

We wake up every morning making positive statements about life. The desire of another person may be sincere but harmful to our lives. The person whose business is the making of coffins may be praying for prosperity. But his prosperity depends on the sales of the coffins. If people don't die, his business will not move forward. Normally, nobody wants to die but to live. You can see how the sincere desires of one person can sincerely hurt another.

Life is full of mysteries and conflicts. There are some desires of yours that are completely detrimental to other human lives. Innocently, you pray for the fulfilment of those desires and wishes and they happen as soon as possible. All these experiences make conflicts very real in life.

CONFLICTING DESIRES

Life is full of mysteries and conflicts. Doctors pray to enjoy patronage in their hospitals, while people pray to escape anything that could take them to the hospital. A lawyer desires to have clients, but people pray to escape troubles in life. How would lawyers survive without conflicts that would take people to court? A prison warder would be jobless without prisoners; but nobody wants to go to the prison for any reason. These are conflicts and serious storms of life.

Desires conflict desires. Some things are set against other things. It is in this constant motion that we live each day of our lives with the mysteries of life getting deeper beyond human comprehension. Only God can save from all conflicts. He alone can deliver from all afflictions of life.

There is someone who has turned the world into a ring of tribulations. He has converted the earth into a place for the tournament of trials and temptations.

He has made the world a place to display tribulations. This person is known as the devil. He is behind the terrible storms of life. Therefore, life is a battle, but when things go wrong, what are you supposed to do? You need to seek victory over all the tribulations of life through Jesus Christ.

CHAPTER Three

Classification of STORMS

We cannot sufficiently examine the issue of storms without attempting their classification.

1. **Self-made storms:** When a woman in our Port Harcourt church, got home after going for deliverance, she borrowed a comb from a neighbour of hers to plait her hair. She had been borrowing the comb for years, but this day, while she put the comb on her laps she suddenly felt something moving on her laps. As she looked, she found a live snake. The comb had become a serpent.

    She then rushed to the church and related her experience. She had been combing her hair with a serpent for years. This is a case of a self-made storm. It could result from ignorance or negligence.

2. **Storms caused by others:** Some storms are caused by others. As we prayed for a sister, we received a revelation that her problem originated from her name. She told us her name, which when

translated means "beautiful snake" and her surname means "wizard gave birth to rebellion." Her storms resulted from the names she didn't give herself.

3. **Storms by the devil:** The devil can directly initiate storms in people's lives. One of my school mates was heading for a first class degree with his very good grades. One day, the devil ministered to him to steal a book from the library. He was a clever boy and knew that everybody would be searched at the library's exit.

    The library was a building of six floors. He took the book to the last floor late at night and threw it out from the window with the intention of picking it downstairs. Unfortunately, someone saw the book, cleverly hid himself and waited for whoever would come to pick it. Soon, this boy came, picked it up and was caught. That was how his beautiful career ended. The devil motivated him to do what he did, and that raised a storm that sank his career.

4. **Storms by God:** Storms can be caused by God as in the case of Jonah. If you flee from God's assignment, He can bring storms upon you. He can cause trouble for you, if you decide to be like Jonah who was told to go to Nineveh and he fled to a different city.

My heart is filled with pity for you, if you have been running away from the call of God. I feel Incidental pity for you who is supposed to be serving God seriously but you have been captured by Delilah.

CHARACTERISTICS OF STORMS OF LIFE

1. **They do not discriminate:** They come upon every man.

2. **We have no control over where and when they hit us:** One old father in the Lord used to tell us that the devil throws stones at everybody; the difference lies in where it hits us.

3. **They don't forewarn before they are let loose:** Storms are very rude visitors. They visited a couple

who had four children. To avoid them from having more children, the man and the woman were operated upon. Incidentally when returning with their four children sitting at the back seat of their car, they had a terrible accident and lost all the four children. That was a storm, a rude visitor.

4. **Storms have no respect for persons nor for the opinion of men.**

5. **There is no age exempted from the storms of life.**

6. **Storms vary with persons:** Your troubles are different from other men's troubles. This is why you can't compare yourself with others.

7. **The storms of life are neither gentle nor soothing:** They can be senselessly violent

8. **The storms of life are like stark illiterate people who know nothing and thus are failing on anything:** A woman, who could not find a husband,

came for deliverance some years ago. She said a herbalist once told her to wear a pant two weeks, remove it after that, put it in a pot and prepare a stew of okro with it, that any man that ate the stew would not be able to go away from her. She did as the herbalist said. The storms of life can be as crude as a stark illiterate person.

9. **The storms of life may destroy everything around you.**

10. **The storms of life may result in drifting**: That is why a pastor could wander away from his ministerial and Christian life into sin.

11. **The storms of life make fake friends to run to you.**

12. **The storms of life can make you better or bitter.**

13. **The storms of life obeys the voice of Jesus**: All manners of storms obey Jesus' voice, no matter the powers behind them.

DIVINE STORMS

God sometimes allows storms into our lives. This kind of storms are not satanic storms. They come as divine accidents which happen by God's permission. Satanic storms are attacks from the devil. Divine storms are meant for our good because they are productive. But satanic storms are destructive.

Divine storms come to us from the loving hands of God. But satanic storms are meant to trap us. Divine storms will not cause us to do evil, but satanic storms often lead you into sin. Divine storms lead us into maturity, but satanic storms leave us bruised, wounded or dead.

The way to deal with divine storms is to repent and be obedient to the Lord. The way to deal with satanic storms is to attack them by rebuking the power behind them. Jesus rebuked the wind and there was a great calm. There was a demonic power behind the wind and that was why the Bible says that Jesus rebuked it.

THE WAY OF VICTORY

To have victory in the storms of life, you must take these steps.

1. Completely surrender your life to Jesus.
2. Confirm your perfect obedience to the Lord and complete any incomplete obedience in your life.
3. Pray against satanic storms.
4. Utter a holy cry unto the Lord.

As a sinner, there is need to confess your sins to God, to invite Jesus into your heart and to surrender to Him completely. As a believer, ask God to forgive you in all areas of life where your obedience is not complete. Ask Him to give you the grace to align yourself to divine orders. Surrender yourself to the authority of His word so that He can calm your storms.

Prayer Points

1. (*Lay your right hand on your head and pray thus:*). Oh Lord, provoke my destiny into breakthrough, in the name of Jesus.

2. Every evil power, attending a daily meeting for my sake, you will not come back home, in the name of Jesus.

3. Every evil power, attending a daily meeting for my sake, I chain you to your place of meeting, in the name of Jesus.

4. Every power that does not want to see my joy, what are you waiting for, die, in the name of Jesus.

5. Any power, reviving bad things in my life, be disgraced in Jesus name.

. Affliction will not rise again in my life in Jesus name.

7. Every handwriting of Affliction, I wipe you off by the power in the blood of Jesus name.

Every power targeted at my peace, be disgraced in Jesus name.

Every alter of affliction prepared for my destiny, I pull you down, in the name of Jesus.

.0. Every power, working against my Good health, I command you to be disgraced in the name of Jesus .

11. I bind and cast out, every oppressive Spirit in Jesus name.

12. I shall not be a victim repeated oppression in Jesus name.

13. My destiny reject every circle of affliction in Jesu name.

14. Spirit of the living God arise in your power and put to shame any power that wants to put me to shame in Jesus name.

15. Holy Ghost fire, burn to ashes every plantation of affliction, in the name of Jesus.

16. Every yoke of the oppressor be broken in Jesus name.

17. My body reject every handwriting of infirmity in Jesus name.

18. My life, reject every handwriting of affliction in Jesus name.

19. I arise by the spirit of God to torment every tormentor and oppress every oppressor in Jesus name

CHAPTER

Four

Provoking your RAINFALL

And Elijah said unto Ahab, Get thee up, eat and drink; for there is a sound of abundance of rain. So Ahab went up to eat and to drink. And Elijah went up to the top of Carmel; and he cast himself down upon the earth, and put his face between his knees, And said to his servant, Go up now, look toward the sea. And he went up, and looked, and said, There is nothing. And he said, Go again seven times. And it came to pass at the seventh time, that he said, Behold, there ariseth a little cloud out of the sea, like a man's hand. And he said, Go up, say unto Ahab, Prepare thy chariot, and get thee down, that the rain stop thee not. And it came to pass in the mean while, that the heaven was black with clouds and wind, and there was a great rain. And Ahab rode, and went to Jezreel. 1Kings18:41-45.

Many people do not know that after a storm comes a rainfall of blessing. God does not expect you to spend all your time battling with storms. He expects you to rise up and provoke your rainfall. When your rainfall is provoked, your moment of celebration comes.

WHAT DOES IT MEAN TO PROVOKE YOUR RAINFALL?

To provoke means to deliberately annoy. It means to incite something to do something. It means to incite by arousing anger. It means to stimulate into action. So, whenever you say 'provoke,' anger is involved.

When we were very little boys, we used to go to play and pluck fruits at a nearby railway compound. One day, somebody took me to the compound and we saw a lot of ripe mangoes and we were throwing stones at them. All of a sudden, we heard the barking of a big dog which was rushing towards us with madness. Prior to that time, I had never climbed a tree, but when I saw the anger and the violence with which the dog was coming, I found

35

myself on a tree. How I got there I did not know. So, something provoked me and I got on top of that tree. You never knew what you could do sometimes until you try.

THE CHALLENGE

I was a teacher for many years in a secondary school. I was the master on duty one day. As a master on duty you would go round to see that all the students were in the classrooms. One would also go round the toilets and everywhere. As I was going round that day, I noticed the head of a student inside the toilet. When I looked down I did not see the person's legs. I then looked from the top and saw a boy kneeling right on top of the water closet and busy reading a letter. He did not see me for about three minutes. By the time he looked up and saw me, he screamed. I said, "Bring that letter." He said, "No sir, no sir, no sir. Don't read this letter."

He gave me the letter with shaking hands. I saw in the first paragraph: "The garden of love, dearest apple of my eye, the sugar in my tea." I said, "In what class are you?"

He said, "Form 3," that is, what we now call JSS III. "Who wrote this letter?" He said, "One girl in Form II." I said, "Go and bring the girl." He said, "Ah master, beat me and let me go." I said, "No beating. Go and bring the girl."

Later he dragged the little girl to me and I said, "You wrote this letter?" She said, "Yes." I said, "Okay, go and bring me your class teacher." She did and the teacher and I looked at the school results to see how well that boy and the girl were doing. I found out that in the last exam, the boy was number three to the last person and the girl was number two to the last. I now said, "Well, if I take you to the principal you know what will happen." They said, "Yes, he will send us out of this school." I said, "I will not do that. Now, you have three weeks to the exams. If your position does not come between number one and number ten, this letter will get to the school authority and both of you will go." They said, "Thank you, sir," and went away. Do you know what? What I did to them provoked them into action. They read very hard and made it.

HOLY PROVOCATION

A sister, who was attending my house fellowship, had a dream where some short demons came to confront her. She said, "I bind all of you, in the name of Jesus." The demons started to laugh and in the end said, "Everybody is binding and you too are binding." When she woke up she was mad with anger and went on dry fast and by the time these demons came again, she was able to deal with them. That was holy provocation.

The Lord has showed me a vision of a cloud of abundance of good rain upon many of His people. Although the cloud was very dark and was supposed to bring rain, no rain was falling. The enemy has removed water from the cloud of many people. They saw the cloud and when they expected the rain to fall, all of a sudden it cleared away.

Beloved, there is restlessness in God's people all over the world now. It appears as if all the children of God all over the world were experiencing one form of frustration or the other. The big truth is that before God can give us more than what we have now, we have to show that we are dissatisfied with the state we are in.

I went to greet an acquaintance who wanted to beat his son to a state of coma because the boy came home with a poor result. The daddy said, "This is a poor result. Look at so, so and so son. Look at our neighbour's son. They did better. You did very poorly. The boy said, "Must I match up to the performance of the boy?" So, the boy was satisfied with his position. God's people should not get used to bondage. Confess this statement: "I shall not get used to any bondage, in the name of Jesus." Children of God should not get comfortable in the tail position. They should never feel at home in bondage.

THE ZERO HOUR

Perhaps, even as you are reading this message, you have arrived at the position which in deliverance we call zero hour. Zero hour is the lowest hour. It is when somebody is totally in a mess, when you are totally down and really need help. It is when somebody is filled with confusion and frustration is reigning. It is when you are at a standstill in life. It is a situation where nothing has been able to help you, a situation where your knowledge and brain have become useless.

The zero hour is a situation where you simply do not know what to do again. It is a situation where your helpers flee and you are on your own, even those you helped in the past are looking at you and not lifting one finger to assist you. It is an hour where everything seems to have failed and your friends are becoming your enemies. A situation where all incomes dry up, the business refuses to move and you are at your wits' end.

It is exactly when human intelligence has terminated and thoughts of a way out have been exhausted. You have done everything you know how to do but there is no solution. Perhaps you have arrived at that situation. But now I tell you that there is a way out. You need to provoke your rainfall. Elijah needed that rain and it would have been a disaster if he had not provoked it. If the rain refuses to fall, you have to take some actions to provoke it.

WHEN YOU NEED TO PROVOKE YOUR RAINFALL

1. When your victory is not complete.
2. When those who are to mock you have gathered.
3. When unbelievers are asking you where your God is.
4. When a satanic audience is waiting for your downfall.
5. When evil powers are challenging God in your life.
6. When you have looked at the whole of your family line and you don't want to follow its evil pattern.
7. When the viper of disgrace that has attached itself to your hand is trying to bite you.
8. When the enemy has sucked you dry.
9. When your debt is mounting and your income is low.
10. When the Lazarus of your destiny has been embalmed and buried.

11. When yokes begin to multiply and chain problems continue to come.
12. When lodge members, occult people and evil assemblies are saying, "You better join us."
13. When you are being encouraged to be disobedient to God because you have a problem.
14. When shedding tears have become your regular affair.
15. When the road you are travelling on is becoming rougher and rougher.
16. When you notice what we call 'finishing fever' in your life. When spiritual fever starts as you are about to finish something.
17. When you are becoming an expert at finishing what you should not have started.
18. When you try to smile and the smile is not coming at all.
19. When your nose is bleeding and your eyes are black in the boxing ring of life.

HOW TO PROVOKE YOUR RAINFALL

There is nobody that God has not programmed a good destiny for. The Bible says, "I know the thoughts that I have towards you, they are the thoughts of good and not of evil." That is what the Bible says, meaning that God does not have terrible or bad destiny for anybody. But the rain of destiny may refuse to fall. How do you speak to the clouds today that they must rain abundance on you? How should you declare that what you have been having are showers of blessing, but now you want the rain to fall?

WHAT TO DO:

1. **Disband worry from your life:** John 14:1 says, *"Let not your heart be troubled."* It does not say, "Pray for God not to allow your heart to be troubled." Worry will give you something to do but it won't get you anywhere. It is not your friend at all. It is your enemy. It cannot be found in God's vocabulary. If you read the Bible very well, you will find that Jesus was never in a hurry.

He knew what He wanted to do and He did it. Anything they said to scare Him did not work.

Worry and faith are incompatible, because immediately worry runs in, faith jumps out. The beginning of worry is the end of faith. We could see that Elijah was not worried at all. He was confident that that rain would fall.

I remember the story of one little girl. There was no rain in their city and the Christians decided to gather to pray that rain would fall. As they were going for the prayer meeting, the girl said, "Daddy, let me follow you." The daddy said she could come along. Later the girl said, "Daddy, wait, I have taken my Bible but there is something I have forgotten." And she ran inside and took an umbrella. The daddy asked her: "What are you doing with the umbrella?" She said, "Daddy, but we are going to pray that God should send rain." The man laughed and said, "Well, it has not rained for many years."

44

They went and before the prayer meeting got half way, rain started. It was only the little girl who had an umbrella.

Worry has nowhere to go and it gets nowhere.

Many years ago, when I was in England, one doctor told me a story that there was one patient crying every night, "Doctor, give me medicine or I will die. Give me medicine or I will die." The patient was screaming and screaming but they had given him all the medicine that he was to take. When he continued to cry, the doctor went and got a sterile water, drew it inside the needle and syringe and injected it on him. He then said, thank you and slept off. So, it was not the sickness that wanted to kill the man, it was worry.

Many die before their time because of worry. I remember the day that all the guests in one hotel deserted the hotel. Somebody was crying in one of the rooms: "It is inside my bag." They knocked at the door of that room but the fellow did not open the door. The other guests started running out thinking that the man wanted to bring out a gun from his bag. But the man was just having a dream.

He later explained that he found himself inside a house in the dream, the door was locked, he wanted to go out and was looking for his keys and was saying, "It is inside my bag." Worry gets nobody anywhere. That is why Jesus said, "Be anxious for nothing but in everything by prayer and supplication, let your request be known unto God." (Philippians 4:6). When you make your request known unto God, His peace will come.

2. **Violent faith:** Elijah said to Ahab, "Go, eat and drink for there is the sign of abundance of rain." There was no physical sign of rain but Elijah had evidence of it inside him. I want you by your ears of faith to hear the sound of your breakthroughs today.

3. **Pray until something happens:** Pray until you feel the drops of rain falling on your body. Don't get up until God answers.

4. **Never accept your present position as final:** The enemy might have been playing games with you. Don't agree with his game. Don't negotiate with him at any level. Don't go to his camp to warm yourself in his fire. Because if you warm yourself in his fire, you will pay for the heat that you enjoy there. The devil operates a primitive trade by barter. Everything anybody gets from him would be paid for. So, don't go to him for help. Also, somebody has said that the greatest enemy of success is present achievement: "Well, I am doing well; I thank God. So, I don't need to do anything more". Don't accept where you are as your final bus-stop. Don't take your financial position now as your final financial bus-stop. Don't take your spiritual life now as your final spiritual bus-stop.

5. **Keep going until you see results:** Elijah said, "Go again, go again, go again." Keep going until you see perfection. Don't allow the enemy to get you depressed. All those periods you spend in sitting down to mourn and in self-sympathy, you allow the enemy to gain on you. If God would open the eyes of some people, instead of sitting down to be crying they will be jumping up and be doing praise worship, because they will see how close they are to what God wants to give them. A lot of us don't understand the principles of God. When you get born again you say, "I want chin-chin and doughnut." He says, 'Take." You say, "That is good. Now, I want goody goody." He says, "Take."

Then as you grow in faith you find that sometimes when you ask for something it will be slow in coming. God is training you to see how firm you can stand. Keep going, don't give up. Keep going, keep going. If you pray and after the prayer doubt comes into your mind again, forget that you have prayed, go back again and pray. All the faith preachers who say, "once you pray once it is okay" are now seeing their mistake. Elijah said, "Go again, go again, go again, go seven times." It was not until the seventh time that some clouds like a little hand came up and then things began to happen.

6. **Draw near to God:** That is, put away anything offensive to Him in your life. Every apple of the devil has worms in it. If the devil gives you a scotch egg to eat, you can be sure that only the flour outside it is good, the egg must be bad. If you draw near to God, He too will draw near to you. If you move away from Him, He too will move farther away from you. And since His legs are longer than your own, if He moves back one step He might have moved 500 miles when you have moved only one foot. Draw near to God.

7. **Pray to provoke a big rainfall:** Elijah used the weapon of prayer to provoke a big rain. Many people

49

are supposed to be employers of labour but they are now being employed. Some don't even have a job. They have to provoke rain and by this very tomorrow begin to see it falling upon them.

Prayer Points

1. I provoke my heavens to open, in the name of Jesus. (*Pray this seven times and shout seven Hallelujah*).

2. Every power that has locked me up, die, in the name of Jesus.

3. My rain of marital, business and career breakthroughs, I provoke you by the blood of Jesus. Fall, in the name of Jesus. (*Please, be specific*).

4. Every power stealing the rain of my blessing, what are you waiting for? Die, in the name of Jesus.

5. Where is the Lord God of Elijah? Provoke my rain of blessing to fall, in the name of Jesus.

6. I terminate the activity of the terminator in Jesus name

7. Oh yoke of the power of death, break in Jesus name.

8. I shall not die but live to declare the works of God in Jesus name.

9. I bind and put to shame every eater of flesh and drinker of blood in the name of Jesus.

10. Every power, that does not want to see me alive loose your hold in the name of Jesus.

11. I shall not absorb my evil arrow that flies by day or by night in the name of Jesus.

12. Let your power, o lord fill my life to the brim in Jesus name.

13. Every ordination of the terminator, I command you to fail, in the name of Jesus.

14. By the power that cut-off the head of Goliath, let the head of the terminator be cut-off in the name of Jesus.

15. I plead to the blood of Jesus over every pronouncement of death fashioned against me In the name of Jesus.

16. Oh glory of God, arise and shine in my life, in Jesus name.

17. Let the rain of blessing fall upon me and quench every terminating fire, in the name of Jesus.

19. You wicked terminators, I bind you and cast you out in the name of Jesus.

20. Every weapon of oppression be destroyed by the fire of the God of Elijah in the name of Jesus.

21. Every power that walks about at night, to wage war against me I burn you alive in Jesus name.

OTHER PUBLICATIONS BY DR. D. K. OLUKOYA

1. 20 Marching Orders To Fulfill Your Destiny
2. 30 Things The Anointing Can Do For You
3. 30 Poverty Destroying Keys
4. 30 Prophetic Arrows From Heaven
5. A-Z of Complete Deliverance
6. Abraham's Children In Bondage
7. Basic Prayer Patterns
8. Be Prepared
9. Bewitchment must die
10. Biblical Principles of Dream Interpretation
11. Biblical Principles of Long Life
12. Born Great, But Tied Down
13. Breaking Bad Habits
14. Breakthrough Prayers For Business Professionals
15. Bringing Down The Power of God
16. Brokenness
17. Can God Trust You?
18. Can God?
19. Command The Morning
20. Connecting to The God of Breakthroughs
21. Consecration Commitment & Loyalty
22. Contending For The Kingdom
23. Criminals In The House Of God
24. Dancers At The Gate of Death
25. Dealing With The Evil Powers of Your Father's House
26. Dealing With Tropical Demons
27. Dealing With Local Satanic Technology
28. Dealing With Witchcraft Barbers
29. Dealing With Unprofitable Roots
30. Dealing With Hidden Curses

31. Dealing With Destiny Vultures
32. Dealing With Satanic Exchange
33. Dealing With Destiny Thieves
34. Deliverance Of The Head
35. Deliverance ,of The Tongue
36. Deliverance: God's Medicine Bottle
37. Deliverance from Evil Load
38. Deliverance From Spirit Husband
39. Deliverance From The Limiting Powers
40. Deliverance From Evil Foundation
41. Deliverance of The Brain
42. Deliverance Of The Conscience
43. Deliverance By Fire
44. Destiny Clinic
45. Destroying Satanic Masks
46. Disgracing Soul Hunters
47. Divine Yellow Card
48. Divine Prescription For Your Total Immunity
49. Divine Military Training
50. Dominion Prosperity
51. Drawers Of Power From The Heavenlies
52. Evil Appetite
53. Evil Umbrella
54. Facing Both Ways
55. Failure In The School Of Prayer
56. Fire For Life's Journey
57. Fire for Spiritual Battles for The 21st Century Army
58. For We Wrestle ...
59. Freedom Indeed
60. Fresh Fire (Bilingual book in French)

61. God's Key To A Happy Home
62. Healing Through Prayers
63. Holiness Unto The Lord
64. Holy Fever
65. Holy Cry
66. Hour Of Decision
67. How To Obtain Personal Deliverance
68. How To Pray When Surrounded By The Enemies
69. I Am Moving Forward
70. Idols Of The Heart
71. Igniting Your Inner Fire
72. Igniting Your Inner Fire
73. Is This What They Died For?
74. Kill Your Goliath By Fire
75. Killing The Serpent of Frustration
76. Let God Answer By Fire
77. Let Fire Fall
78. Limiting God
79. Looking Unto Jesus
80. Lord, Behold Their Threatening Madness of The Heart
81   Making Your Way Through The
82. Traffic Jam of Life
83. Meat For Champions
84. Medicine For Winners
85. My Burden For The Church
86. Open Heavens Through Holy Disturbance
87. Overpowering Witchcraft
88. Passing Through The Valley of The Shadow of Death
89. Paralysing The Riders And The Horse
90. Personal Spiritual Check-Up

91. Possessing The Tongue of Fire
92. Power To Recover Your Birthright
93. Power Against Captivity
94. Power Against Coffin Spirits
95. Power Against Unclean Spirits
96. Power Against The Mystery of Wickedness
97. Power Against Destiny Quenchers
98. Power Against Dream Criminals
99. Power Against Local Wickedness
100. Power Against Marine Spirits
101. Power Against Spiritual Terrorists
102. Power To Recover Your Lost Glory
103. Power To Disgrace The Oppressors
104. Power Must Change Hands
105. Power Must Change Hands (Prayer Points from 1995-2010)
106. Power To Shut Satanic Doors
107. Power Against The Mystery of Wickedness
108. Power of Brokenness
109. Pray Your Way To Breakthroughs
110. Prayer To Make You Fulfill Your Divine Destiny
111. Prayer Strategies For Spinsters And Bachelors
112. Prayer Warfare Against 70 Mad Spirits
113. Prayer Is The Battle
114. Prayer To Kill Enchantment
115. Prayer Rain
116. Prayers To Destroy Diseases And Infirmities
117. Prayers For Open Heavens
118. Prayers To Move From Minimum To
119. Praying Against Foundational Poverty
120. Praying Against The Spirit Of The Valley

121. Praying In The Storm
122. Praying To Dismantle Witchcraft
123. Praying To Destroy Satanic Roadblocks
124. Principles of Conclusive Prayers
125. Principles Of Prayer
126. Raiding The House of The Strongman
127. Release From Destructive Covenants
128. Revoking Evil Decrees
129. Safeguarding Your Home
130. Satanic Diversion of the Black Race
131. Secrets of Spiritual Growth & Maturity
132. Self-Made Problems (Bilingual book in French)
133. Seventy Rules of Spiritual Warfare
134. Seventy Sermons To Preach To Your Destiny
135. Silencing The Birds Of Darkness
136. Slave Masters
138. Smite The Enemy And He Will Flee
139. Speaking Destruction Unto The Dark Rivers
140. Spiritual Education
141. Spiritual Growth And Maturity
142. Spiritual Warfare And The Home
143. Stop Them Before They Stop You
144. Strategic Praying
145. Strategy Of Warfare Praying
146. Students In The School Of Fear
147. Symptoms Of Witchcraft Attack
148. Taking The Battle To The Enemy's Gate
149. The Amazing Power of Faith
150. The God of Daniel (Bilingual book in French)
151. The God of Elijah (Bilingual book in French)

152. The Vagabond Spirit
153. The Unlimited God
154. The Wealth Transfer Agenda
155. The Way Of Divine Encounter
156. The Unconquerable Power
157. The Baptism of Fire
158. The Battle Against The Spirit Of Impossibility
159. The Chain Breaker
160. The Dinning Table Of Darkness
161. The Enemy Has Done This
162. The Evil Cry Of Your Family Idol
163. The Fire Of Revival
164. The School of Tribulation
165. The Gateway To Spiritual Power
166. The Great Deliverance
167. The Internal Stumbling Block
168. The Lord Is A Man Of War
169. The Mystery Of Mobile Curses
170. The Mystery Of The Mobile Temple
171. The Prayer Eagle
172. The University of Champions
173. The Power of Aggressive Prayer Warriors
174. The Power of Priority
175. The Tongue Trap
176. The Terrible Agenda
177. The Scale of The Almighty
178. The Hidden Viper
179. The Star In Your Sky
180. The Star Hunters
181. The Spirit Of The Crab

182.   The Snake In The Power House
183.   The Slow Learners
184.   The University of Champions
185.   The Skeleton In Your Grandfather's Cupboard
186.   The Serpentine Enemies
187.   The Secrets Of Greatness
188.   The Seasons Of Life
189.   The Pursuit Of Success
190.   Tied Down In The Spirits
191.   Too Hot To Handle
192.   Turnaround Breakthrough
193.   Unprofitable Foundations
194.   Victory Over Your Greatest Enemies
195.   Victory Over Satanic Dreams
196.   Violent Prayers Against Stubborn Situations
197.   War At The Edge Of Breakthroughs
198.   Wasted At The Market Square of Life
199.   Wasting The Wasters
200.   Wealth Must Change Hands
201.   What You Must Know About The House Fellowship
202.   When the Battle is from Home
203.   When You Need A Change
204.   When The Deliverer Need Deliverance
205.   When Things Get Hard
206.   When You Are Knocked Down
207.   When You Are Under Attack
208.   When The Enemy Hides
209.   When God Is Silent
210.   Where Is Your Faith
211.   While Men Slept

212. Woman! Thou Art Loosed.
213. Why Problems Come Back
214. Your Battle And Your Strategy
215. Your Foundation And Destiny
216. Your Mouth And Your Deliverance
217. Your Mouth and Your Warfare

YORUBA PUBLICATIONS
1. Adura Agbayora
2. Adura Ti Nsi Oke Ni dii
3. Ojo Adura

FRENCH PUBLICATIONS
1. Pluie De Priere
2. Espirit De Vagabondage
3. En Finir Avec Les Forces Malefiques De La Maison De Ton Pere
4. Que l'envoutement Perisse
5. Frappez l'adversaire Et Il Fuira
6. Comment Recevior La Delivrance Du Mari Et De La Femme De Nuit
7. Comment Se Delivrer Soi-meme
8. Pouvoir Contre Les Terrorites Spirituels
9. Priere De Percees Pour Les Hommes D'affaires
10. Prier Jusqu'a Remporter La Victoire
11. Prieres Violentes Pour Humilier Les Problsmes Opiniatres
12. Priere Pour Detruire Les Maladies Et Les Infirmites
13. Le Combat Spirituel Et Le Foyer
14. Bilan Spirituel Personnel
15. Victoires Sur Les Reves Sataniques
16. Prieres De Combat Contre 70 Esprits Dechalnes
17. La Deviation Satanique De La Race Noire

18. Ton Combat Et Ta Strategie
19. Votre Fondement Et Votre Destin
20. Revoquer Les Decrets Malefiques
21. Cantique Des Coritiques
22. Le Mauvais Cri Des Idoles
23. Quand Les Choses Deviennent Difficiles
24. Les Strategies De Prieres Pour Les Celibataires
25. Se Liberer Des Alliances Malefiques
26. Demanteler La Sorcellerie
27. La Deliverance: Le Flacon De Medicament De Dieu
28. La Deliverance De La Tete
29. Commander Le Matin
30. Ne Grand Mais Lie
31. Pouvoir Contre Les Demons Tropicaux
32. Le Programme De Tranfert Des Richesse
33. Les Etudiants A l'ecole De La Peur
34. L'etoile Dans Votre Ciel
35. Les Saisons De La Vie
36. Femme Tu Es Liberee

OTHER PUBLICATIONS BY PASTOR(MRS) SHADE OLUKOYA

1. Power to Fulfil Your Destiny
2. Principles of A Successful Marriage
3. The Call of God
4. The Daughters of Phillip
5. Violence Against Negative Voices
6. Woman of Wonder
7. When Your Destiny is Under Attack
8. I decree an uncommon change

ALL OBTAINABLE AT:

The Battle Cry Christian Ministries-
322, Herbert Macaulay Street, Sabo, Yaba.
P. O. Box 12272, Ikeja, Lagos
Telephone: 08033044239, 01-8044415

MFM International Bookshop
13, Olasimbo Street, Onike-Yaba, Lagos

All MFM Church Branches nationwide
and leading Christian Bookstores

BOOK ORDER

Is there any book by
Dr. D. K. Olukoya
(General Overseer MFM Ministries)
that you would like to have?

Have you seen his latest books?
To place an order for this End-Time Materials,
Call: 08161229775

Battle Cry Ministries... *Equipping the saints of God.*

God bless.

The Book

Naturally, it is easy to identify a person in your neighborhood whom you can describe as rich and wealthy. The next possible tendency on your part is to consider him as someone who has no problems (storms). This is because the common erroneous benchmark is to measure success by ones wealth. Definitely, this is not so. With all he may have, he has one or more problems (storms) agitating his mind which his money cannot solve and requires a divine intervention.

On page 5 of this book is a list of a wide range of the storms one can encounter in life. On page 19 are facts above the 7Ds that facilitate storms in life.

The beauty of divine security against the storms of life is contained in Ps 34: 19-20, in addition to this is the fact that when you focus on God, you have nothing to worry about as written in John 14:1.

To quote the author, "Difficulties are the forerunners of greatness. Passing through hard times will give you the spiritual muscles you will need later in life.

By the time you read the last chapter of this book, you will have been armed with how to withstand any storm in life. You are given a guideline on how to provoke your heaven to open and enjoy your victory.

The Author

Dr. D. K. Olukoya is the General Overseer of the Mountain of Fire and Miracles Ministries and The Battle Cry Christian Ministries.

The Mountain of Fire and Miracles Ministries' Headquarters is the largest single Christian congregation in Africa with attendance of over 120,000 in any Church service.

MFM is a full gospel ministry devoted to the revival of Apostolic signs, Holy Ghost Fireworks, miracle and the unlimited demonstration of the power of God to deliver to the uttermost. Absolute holiness within and without as spiritual insecticide and pre-requisite for heaven is openly taught. MFM is a do-it-yourself Gospel Ministry, where your hands are trained to wage war and your fingers to do battle.

Dr. Olukoya holds a first class honours degree in Micro-biology from the University of Lagos and a PhD in Molecular Genetics from the University of Reading, United Kingdom. As a researcher, he has over seventy scientific publications to his credit.

Anointed by God, Dr. Olukoya is a prophet, evangelist, teacher and preacher of the Word. His life and that of his wife, Shade and their son Elijah Toluwani are living proofs that all power belongs to God.

ISBN: 978-978-920-039-9

www.ingramcontent.com/pod-product-compliance
Lightning Source LLC
LaVergne TN
LVHW051200080426
835508LV00021B/2727